Your Fade

The Corner of Safe and Never Made It

Your Fade

The Corner of Safe and Never Made It

E.C. Bolster

PHASE EIGHT PUBLISHING
P8

Your Fade: The Corner of Safe and Never Made It

ISBN: 978-0-9989852-7-5

Published by Phase Eight Publishing,
an imprint of Phase Seven Comics.
Alec Longstreth, Editor.

https://www.phasesevencomics.com/phase8/

Special Thanks:
Gab, CR, and Jaim

Table of Contents

Your Fade   3

Boy Wonder   5

For The Birds   7

Minds Of Men   9

His Best Bukowski   11

Glass Blown Men   13

This Page   15

The Science Of Growing Gorgeous   17

Even After   19

Masterpiece   21

Love On Paper   23

Golden Ratio   25

Between Kisses   27

The Women I Be   29

Long Blue Winter   31

The Poet's Drug Of Choice   33

Homecoming   35

Wine and Smoke   37

Chasing Different Dragons   39

Stagger Home Alone Roulette   41

Until Now   43

for Joe

Your Fade

I woke early
to feel you
finally go dark
So I'll lean back on my hands
and mourn your fade
just this once
Cross-legged in the sand
on a Mexican beach at dawn
and recall you only
until the sun comes up

Boy Wonder

Only five when his father died
How does little boy make sense
of black lists, polio
or mothers who've gone mad
How does he tell the books
meant for burial
from ones that stay on the shelf
Why she's gone where
The Outside locks its doors
and the paper cups serve pills
When she promised him
she'd save the world
and why she never will

For The Birds

I don't write birds
Because my dad
wrote them a lot when
he was losing his edge
When he no longer
fought for anything
but the afternoon
and a glass of wine
Feet upon
his new deck chair
he found
for a great deal
at 'Freddies'
Waking from naps
to refill his glass
Unless he could get
my step mom to do it
And then he would
write about her ankles

But today
Today I could write
a poem
for the birds

Minds Of Men

A world's knowledge mastered
at my mother's expense
He took to stages
framed with captive audience
pontificated his craft
for the accolade and applause
Amassed pretty ideas in pretty books
in his own handsome head
Re-packaged them on more pretty paper
A dictator with a pretty title
he gifted them to his people
as if it had never been done
On the isle of Nothing Left To Teach Me
Where the world re-masters
the minds of men

His Best Bukowski

My father does his best Bukowski
All red wine teeth and rage
bared against ideals he once fought
for drunken arguments sake
To cut the jade
an inspired man suffers
When his soul no longer lives
paycheck to paycheck
When he no longer stands up
Objects conscientious against war
indiscriminate death
or the right all men should possess
to grow their hair long

Glass Blown Men

He is the same 2 hundred 85 pound
6 foot 4 eggshell of a man
he's always been
A real life Humpty Dumpty
Clinging by his fingernails
to the crumbling reign of his glory
To college football and a time
when he still had hair
Pecks instead of breasts
When his fists were allowed to solve things
and no one cared how many noses he broke
or that he beat me
Oh how he laments
the good old days
The way all
glass blown men do

This Page

This page marks
the last thoughts
I will have of you tonight
I refuse
to lay awake to you
Fall asleep to the recall
of your voice on loop
I'll allow you no more
of my dreams
My arms will not reach for
or wish themselves around you
I am not
empty with your absence
nor will I
fill at your return
Tonight I refuse
to love you

The Science Of Growing Gorgeous

If what they say is true
and the most beautiful people
are the most broken
Then I am a fucking Goddess
King, queen, prince and princess
I've earned my station
built my throne
Made my crown
by choosing the shiniest pieces
of every shattered version of me
Each sparkle of my eyes forged
from my darkest moments
Every peal of laughter
keeps them in mind
Even when my heart is light
I am still my own Mary Shelly
Dr. Frankenstein genius
who's simply figured out the science
of growing gorgeous
from the things that killed me

Even After

Even after
The ones we will not name
The things we can not speak aloud
and the lengths of our years without

You leave me
a quiet glass of water
should I wake thirsty for you

Masterpiece

I will not know poems
until you've penned yours
inside me
I will not know prose
until we've written
pages and pages
by calling out
each others names
And I will never know poetry
until the morning I wake to you
and the masterpiece
we've made of us

Love On Paper

Laying on your chest
my coffee cup resting on your stomach
your hands turn the pages
fingers point out all the bright places
we should be together
Their colorful gloss lives
the same way we do
Our love so pretty
on paper

Golden Ratio

He says, "If you were an equation you'd be the Golden Ratio."
And I want to listen but his hands
are covered in scars and calluses of the hard working
kind of patience I've never mastered
filtering out the drip of his voice
the old fashioned red bandana in the back
pocket of his blue jeans cuffed at the bottom
The wolf in his eyes and the crows feet
that prove the kind of man he is
the way his hair begs my hand to run it through
the fade of his black t-shirts when they pull
just so over the muscles that swing his hammer
and paddle out past the breakers
where he searches the ocean for meaning
the good waves and the wet salt kisses
that say, "See? I came back safe "
"1.618 is the numerical representation…" he's saying
But I can only watch his lips plump around the math
So I silence him with a kiss the power of gold

Between Kisses

He still sleeps in my bed with me
Forever sixteen we
gave each other things
no one else would
Told each other the truth
in between kisses
we lied too
Spent our nights pretending
okay existed
and the mornings remembering
it doesn't

The Women I Be

If there was such a thing as fair
I'd no longer be
all the women falsely accused
Loved so hard they were abused
Black and blue rape
the color of love
spat in their face
Night and I would reconcile
and he'd stop making me
all these women I've been
All these women I be
He might even let me sleep

Long Blue Winter

All day I've tried
to recall you
All night convey your specifics
and make metaphors of you
in the dark
There's only you
in the center of me
A heat it will take
the slow burn
of the long blue winter
to find words for

The Poet's Drug Of Choice

A muse is just poetic novocaine
A lidocaine synthetic compound
made to numb the pain
with the heroin of lust and late night
Early mornings if you prefer the hard stuff
Write her name in white lines of cocaine
cursive on the same mirror
you wrote all the others
all the nights before
She's just the new
for now muse
Until you find someone else
who gets you higher
Who's easier to use

Homecoming

Decorated and buttoned down
white hat in white hands
End of days setting hot
on clean cornered shoulders
heavy with marine colored gold
Shadow faced and uniform tall
he stands practicing ghost
for an afterlife
only a soldier can see

Wine And Smoke

A tipsy
half way writer
Half drunk
or half on fire
In a world
already too full
of would be poets
wine and smoke

Chasing Different Dragons

In the novocaine weeks
we mistook for love we broke
through writers block walls
Filled our minds with nothing
but the need for each other and the words
that filled our veins in perfect combination
When we could not tangle our bodies
we spoke of the ways we would
When we could not speak
we scrawled our minds manic
pen and paper desperate
to find the inside of one another
Until we mused each other numb
smothered the fire we lusted after
Left each other cold
used up and alone
to chase different dragons

Stagger Home Alone Roulette

Sometimes I like to make
a low cut top
short skirt
five inch high heel wager
Drink way too much
until much too late
and then go for a round of
stagger home alone roulette
Play chicken with the truth
and dare humanity
to prove me wrong

Until Now

The killing happened the night
we parted ways at the corner
of safe and never made it
to warm tucked beneath the covers
our parents bought for us
kept in the homes
we bought for ourselves
We had such good luck
The good fortune to grow up
only sexually assaulted
raped but not murdered
Until now

E.C. Bolster

E.C. was raised on romantic ideas, practical food, and red wine. She lives in secrecy until she decides to be seen, in which case you can't miss her. She has one (human) child.

https://www.instagram.com/ecbolsterlit/